ADJECTIVES

BRAVE BRAVE

CALM CALM

FAITHFUL FAITHFUL

EAGER EAGER

AMBITIOUS AMBITIOUS

DELIGHTFUL
DELIGHTFUL

Write sentences using words from above:

1. ....

2. ....

3. ....

4. ....

5. ....

ADVERBS

AMAZINGLY

AMAZINGLY

ANGRILY ANGRILY

ADVERSELY

ADVERSELY

MOUSE MOUSE

ELEPHANT ELEPHANT

Write sentences using words from above:

1.

2.

3.

4.

5.

ANIMALS

CAT CAT

BAT BAT

DOG DOG

DUCK DUCK

ARROGANTLY

ARROGANTLY

ACTUALLY ACTUALLY

ACCUSINGLY

ACCUSINGLY

Write sentences using words from above:

1. ____

2. ____

3. ____

4. ____

5. ____

BEACH

Name: ___________________

Date: ___________

OCEAN OCEAN

WIND WIND

SUN SUN

HAPPY HAPPY

FAMILY FAMILY

SAND CASTLE SAND
CASTLE

Write sentences using words from above:

1.

2.

3.

4.

5.

FAMILY

FATHER FATHER

MOTHER MOTHER

DAUGHTER DAUGHTER

SON SON

GRANDFATHER

GRANDFATHER

GRANDMOTHER

GRANDMOTHER

Write sentences using words from above:

1.

2.

3.

4.

5.

FARM ANIMALS

DEER DEER

DONKEY DONKEY

DOVE DOVE

DUCK DUCK

COW COW
CHICKEN CHICKEN

Write sentences using words from above:

1. ____

2. ____

3. ____

4. ____

5. ____

FLOWERS

ORCHIDS ORCHIDS

JASMINE JASMINE

ROSE ROSE

DAISY DAISY

TULIPS TULIPS

IRIS IRIS

Write sentences using words from above:

1. ____

2. ____

3. ____

4. ____

5. ____

FRIENDS

FUN FUN

LOVE LOVE

UNDERSTANDING
UNDERSTANDING

HAPPY HAPPY

EXCITING EXCITING

Write sentences using words from above:

1.

2.

3.

4.

5.

JEWELRY

Name: _______________________

Date: _______________

NECKLACES

NECKLACES

RINGS RINGS

EARRINGS EARRINGS

BRACELETS BRACELETS

BROOCHES BROOCHES BROOCHES

Write sentences using words from above:

1.

2.

3.

4.

5.

MONTHS

JANUARY JANUARY

FEBRUARY FEBRUARY

MARCH MARCH

APRIL APRIL

MAY MAY

JUNE JUNE

Write sentences using words from above:

1.

2.

3.

4.

5.

NATURAL DISASTERS

Name: _______________

Date: _______________

EARTHQUAKES

EARTHQUAKES

VOLCANOES

VOLCANOES

LANDSLIDES

LANDSLIDES

WILDFIRES WILDFIRES

DROUGHTS DROUGHTS

FLOODING FLOODING

Write sentences using words from above:

1.

2.

3.

4.

5.

NATURAL RESOURCES

SUNLIGHT SUNLIGHT

SOIL SOIL

WATER WATER

OIL OIL

COAL COAL

NATURAL GAS
NATURAL GAS

Write sentences using words from above:

1.

2.

3.

4.

5.

PARTY

PARTY HAT PARTY

HAT

BALLOONS BALLOONS

CAKE CAKE

CLOWN CLOWN

GIFTS GIFTS

FRIENDS FRIENDS

Write sentences using words from above:

1. ____

2. ____

3. ____

4. ____

5. ____

SPORTS

SOCCER SOCCER

TENNIS TENNIS

BASEBALL BASEBALL

GOLF GOLF

RUNNING RUNNING

Write sentences using words from above:

1.

2.

3.

4.

5.

TOYS

BALL BALL

DOLL DOLL

CAR CAR

TEDDY BEAR TEDDY
BEAR

KITE KITE

ROCKING HORSE
ROCKING HORSE

Write sentences using words from above:

1.

2.

3.

4.

5.

VERBS

DRINK DRINK

EAT EAT

FALL FALL

FEEL FEEL

WORK WORK

STUDY STUDY

Write sentences using words from above:

1. ____

2. ____

3. ____

4. ____

5. ____